PUBLISH YOUR BOOKS ON AMAZON

10 EASY STEPS

BY: KIMBERLY NEPTUNE

Author by: Kimberly Neptune
Published by: Butterfly Thoughts LLC

Title: Publish Your Books on Amazon

Copyright 2023 By: Butterfly Thoughts LLC
All rights reserved.

ISBN # 979-8-9868071-4-0

Content

1 -   Step 1: Log In
5 -   Step 2: Start
7 -   Step 3: Information
9 -   Step 4: Upload 1
12 -   Step 5: Keywords
15 -   Step 6: Upload 2
17 -   Step 7: Price & Royalty
20 -   Step 8: Review
22 -   Step 9: Publish
24 -   Step 10: Promote
27 -   Bonus : ISBN number

Step: 1

Log In

LOG IN TO YOUR AMAZON KDP ACCOUNT.

Do you have an Amazon KDP account?

NO:

To create an account with KDP (Kindle Direct Publishing) on Amazon, go to the KDP website and click on "Sign in" at the top right corner. Then, click on "Create your KDP account". Follow the instructions to fill out your personal information, such as your name, email address, and password. Once you have completed the form, click "Create Account" and you will be ready to start publishing your books on Amazon.

YES:

Once you have logged in to your Amazon KDP (Kindle Direct Publishing) account, you will have access to a range of tools and resources to help you publish and promote your eBook.
By logging in to your Amazon KDP account, you are one step closer to getting your eBook published and reaching a wider audience.

Here are some things you can do once you're logged in:

-
- Create a new eBook project or edit an existing one Upload your manuscript and cover file Set your pricing and royalty options Choose which distribution channels you want to use Monitor your sales and royalties Access marketing and promotional tools, such as Amazon Advertising and Kindle Countdown Deals

Publish your book on Amazon   10 Steps

Step: 2

Start

CLICK ON "CREATE A NEW TITLE" TO START THE BOOK CREATION PROCESS.

Once you have clicked on "Create a New Title," you will be prompted to enter the title of your book. This is an important step, as it will be the first thing readers see when they come across your book. Make sure to choose a catchy and descriptive title that accurately represents the content of your book.

After entering the title, you will then be asked to provide additional information such as the author's name, book description, and cover image. It's important to take the time to craft a compelling book description that will entice readers to want to learn more about your book.

Additionally, choose a cover image that is visually appealing and relevant to the content of your book.

Once you have completed these steps, you will be ready to move onto the next stage of the book creation process.

Step: 3

Information

ENTER THE BOOK'S TITLE, SUBTITLE, AND AUTHOR NAME.

To make sure your book is easily recognizable, it's important to have a clear and concise title, subtitle, and author name. Here are some tips to keep in mind:

- Choose a title that accurately reflects the content of the book and catches the reader's attention.
- If your book covers a specific topic, consider adding a subtitle to provide additional context and entice potential readers.
- Make sure the author name is spelled correctly and is easy to read.

Once you have all this information, you can add it to the cover of your book or the information page. Good luck with your new book!

Step: 4

Upload 1

UPLOAD YOUR BOOK MANUSCRIPT IN A SUPPORTED FORMAT (E.G. WORD, PDF).

Here are some additional points to keep in mind when uploading your book manuscript:
- Make sure the file is complete and error-free before uploading.
- Check that the formatting is consistent throughout the document.
- If you're submitting a PDF, ensure that all fonts are embedded and that the file is optimized for web viewing.
- Consider adding a title page and table of contents to your manuscript to make it easier for readers to navigate.
- If your manuscript includes images or other non-text elements, make sure they are high quality and appear where they are intended to in the document.

By taking the time to ensure that your manuscript is well-prepared before uploading, you can increase the likelihood of it being accepted by publishers or online distributors. Good luck with your writing!

Step: 5

Keywords

CHOOSE THE BOOK'S CATEGORIES AND KEYWORDS TO HELP READERS FIND IT.

When it comes to publishing a book, choosing the right categories and keywords is crucial to make it discoverable to potential readers. Here are some tips to help you select the best ones:
- Research the categories and keywords that are relevant to your book's genre and subject matter. Look at the categories
- and keywords that successful books in your genre are using. Use specific and descriptive
- keywords that accurately reflect the content of your book. Avoid using broad or generic
- keywords that will make your book harder to find. Consider using niche categories and
- keywords that will help your book stand out in a crowded market.

- Regularly review and update your book's categories and keywords to ensure they are still relevant and effective.

By taking the time to carefully select the right categories and keywords, you can increase the visibility of your book and make it easier for readers to find and enjoy.

Step: 6

Upload 2

UPLOAD A BOOK COVER IMAGE THAT MEETS AMAZON'S GUIDELINES.

Here are some additional pieces of information that might be helpful for you while uploading a book cover image on Amazon:

- Amazon requires that the cover image be in a JPEG or TIFF file format.
- The image should be at least 1000 pixels on the longest side.
- The file size of the image should be less than 50MB.
- The cover image should be of high-quality and resolution, with a minimum of 72 dpi (dots per inch).
- The cover image should not contain any pornographic or offensive material.

Ensuring that your cover image meets these guidelines is important for making your book stand out and attract potential readers. A visually appealing and professional-looking cover image can make a big difference in the success of your book on Amazon.

Step: 7

Price & Royalty

SET THE BOOK'S PRICE AND ROYALTY OPTIONS.

To set the price of your book, you need to take into account several factors, such as the production cost, the perceived value of your content, and the prices of similar books in your genre. You also need to decide on the currency and the pricing model (e.g. fixed price vs dynamic pricing). Keep in mind that the price you set will affect the demand for your book, the revenue you can generate, and the perception of your brand. Royalty options refer to the percentage of the book's revenue that you as the author or publisher will receive for each sale. This can vary depending on the distribution channel (e.g. Amazon, Barnes & Noble, your own website), the format (e.g. ebook, print), and the deal you have negotiated with the retailer or distributor.

Some platforms offer different royalty rates for different price ranges or regions, so it's important to read the terms and conditions carefully and do the math to see which option is best for you.

If you're self-publishing your book, you have the freedom to choose both the price and the royalty options. However, you also bear the responsibility of promoting your book, managing the sales, and handling the legal and financial aspects. Make sure you have a solid marketing plan, a professional cover and layout, and a clear understanding of the tax and copyright laws in your jurisdiction.

You may also want to consider hiring a literary agent or a book coach to guide you through the process and increase your chances of success.

Step: 8

Preview

PREVIEW AND APPROVE THE BOOK'S CONTENT AND FORMATTING.

Consider these points when previewing and approving the book's content and formatting:
- Check for consistency in formatting, such as font type, size, and spacing.
- Ensure that headings and subheadings are consistent and properly formatted.
- Look for any spelling or grammar errors and correct them.
- Ensure that images and graphics are high quality and properly placed.
- Verify that all page numbers and chapter titles are correct.
- Check that the table of contents is accurate and properly formatted.
- Make sure that footnotes or endnotes are properly cited and formatted.

By carefully reviewing and approving the book's content and formatting, you can ensure that it is polished and ready for publication.

Step: 9

Publish

CLICK "PUBLISH YOUR KINDLE EBOOK" TO MAKE IT AVAILABLE FOR SALE.

PUBLISH

Once you have clicked "Publish Your Kindle eBook", you can sit back and relax as your book becomes available for sale on Amazon's Kindle store. Here are some things to keep in mind as you wait for your book to reach readers:

- Amazon will take a percentage of the sale price as a commission, so be sure to price your book accordingly.
- Consider promoting your book through social media and other channels to increase its visibility and attract potential readers.
- Keep an eye on your sales and reviews to see how your book is performing and make any necessary updates or changes.
- Don't forget to continue writing and publishing to build your author platform and grow your readership.

Step: 10

Promote

PROMOTE YOUR BOOK AND TRACK ITS SALES USING AMAZON KDP'S MARKETING TOOLS.

As a self-published author, it can be challenging to get your book in front of potential readers. Luckily, Amazon KDP offers a variety of marketing tools to help boost your book's visibility and sales. Here are some ways you can use these tools to promote your book:

- Run a Kindle Countdown Deal: This promotion allows you to offer your book at a discounted price for a limited time, which can entice readers to make a purchase.
- Use Amazon Advertising: With Amazon Advertising, you can create targeted ads for your book that will appear in search results and on product pages. This can help increase your book's visibility to the right audience.

- Utilize Kindle Unlimited: By enrolling your book in Kindle Unlimited, readers can borrow and read your book for free as part of their subscription. This can lead to more exposure and potentially more sales.

In addition to these tools, Amazon KDP also provides sales data and analytics to help you track your book's performance. This information can be invaluable in making informed decisions about future marketing strategies. With Amazon KDP's marketing tools and resources, you can take control of promoting your book and reaching a wider audience.

Publish your book on Amazon   10 Steps

One more thing that you are going to need for you book. In order to fully publish your book you will need ISBN. What is an ISBN?
An ISBN (International Standard Book Number) is a unique identifier assigned to books and other publications to facilitate their identification and tracking. It consists of 13 digits and is used internationally. This number is usually found at the bottom or the top of the bar code.

Where can you get an ISBN?
There are 2 main ways to get an ISBN, either through Amazon or Bowker. Amazon ISBNs are free and are unique identification numbers assigned by Amazon to books that are sold on their platform. While Bowker ISBNs are not free but are globally recognized identification numbers assigned to books by Bowker. Bowker is the official ISBN agency for the United States. Bowker ISBNs can be used to distribute books to multiple retailers, while Amazon ISBNs are specific to Amazon.

Scan or click
on QR code
to get ISBN

Kimberly "KimmyB" Neptune is the owner of Butterfly Thoughts LLC. Kimberly is an Perspective Coach, Speaker and an Author. She is a Trinidadian Caribbean woman born in Brooklyn, New York. She is a beautiful soul with a warm smile, touch and a caring heart. KimmyB's mission is to encourage, motivate and empower human butterflies to heal their broken wings so they can soar in the greatness.

Scan or click here for more

You can find me at:

iambutterflythought

Butterfly Chronicles with Kimmy

 butterflythoughtsllc.com

To be the first to know what is new scan or click here

www.ingramcontent.com/pod-product-compliance
Lightning Source LLC
Chambersburg PA
CBHW060904050426
42453CB00010B/1568